Contents

Section 1	Test 1	Comprehension	
	Test 2	Grammar and punctuation	6
	Test 3	Spelling and vocabulary	8
	Test 4	Comprehension	10
	Test 5	Grammar and punctuation	12
	Test 6	Spelling and vocabulary	14
Section 2	Test 1	Comprehension	16
	Test 2	Grammar and punctuation	18
	Test 3	Spelling and vocabulary	20
	Test 4	Comprehension	22
	Test 5	Grammar and punctuation	24
	Test 6	Spelling and vocabulary	26
Section 3	Test 1	Comprehension	28
	Test 2	Grammar and punctuation	30
	Test 3	Spelling and vocabulary	32
	Test 4	Comprehension	34
	Test 5	Grammar and punctuation	36
	Test 6	Spelling and vocabulary	38
Progress chart			40

A **pull-out answers section** (pages A1 to A12) appears in the centre of this book, between pages 20 and 21. It also gives simple guidance on how best to use this book. Remove this section before the child begins working through the tests.

Section 1 Test 1

Comprehension

Target time: **10 minutes**

Read the text and answer the questions below.

Wonder World Holiday Brochure

Set your imagination on fire with a visit to Wonder World Resort – the most exciting place on Earth! With four fun-packed theme parks that are bursting with the planet's most magical characters and awe-inspiring rides, you'll be blown away. Read on to find out more about what each park has to offer.

Magical Realm

5 Enter a world where dreams come true and fairy tales become reality at the Magical Realm theme park. Marvel at the beautiful Wonder World Castle, gasp at the spectacular firework displays, be entertained by the fantastic parades and meet all your favourite Wonder World characters across five zones that offer hours of fun for all ages.

Animal Kingdom

10 Experience the wild side of Wonder World as you get up close and personal with some of Earth's most fascinating wildlife. Enjoy heart-stopping rides, fabulous shows and breathtaking animal encounters as you embark on an unforgettable safari adventure.

Wonder World Studios

Lose yourself in the magic of cinema and be amazed as your most beloved blockbusters come to life
15 before your eyes at Wonder World Studios. Immerse yourself in any one of our 35 thrilling attractions and experience the glitz and glamour of life as a movie star.

Splash and Slide

Splash, slide and ride your way to a good time at the water park that blows all other water parks out of the water! Experience white-knuckle rides, giant waterslides, enormous wave pools and more.
20 And when you've had enough of all that excitement, relax by the infinity pool or float on the water on a giant lilo – the perfect end to an exhilarating day.

Write **A**, **B**, **C** or **D** on the answer line.

1. At which park might you see fireworks?
   A Magical Realm
   B Animal Kingdom
   C Wonder World Studios
   D Splash and Slide

   _____ /1

2. At which park could you experience life as a movie star?
   A Magical Realm
   B Animal Kingdom
   C Wonder World Studios
   D Splash and Slide

   _____ /1

3. At which park would you be likely to get wet?
   A Magical Realm
   B Animal Kingdom
   C Wonder World Studios
   D Splash and Slide

   _____ /1

4. What is the purpose of this text?
   A to entertain children
   B to persuade people to visit Wonder World
   C to give people a balanced view of Wonder World
   D to tell people how to get to Wonder World

   _____ /1

English
Rapid Tests 4

Siân Goodspeed

Schofield & Sims

Introduction

This book gives you practice in answering English questions quickly.

The questions are like the questions on the 11+ and other school selection tests. You must find the correct answers.

School selection tests are usually timed, so you need to get used to working quickly. Each test has a target time for you to work towards. You should time how long you spend on each test, or you can ask an adult to time you.

What you need

- A pencil
- An eraser
- A clock, watch or stopwatch
- An adult to help you work out how long you take and to mark the test for you

What to do

- Turn to **Section 1 Test 1** on page 4. Look at the grey box at the top of the page labelled **Target time**. This tells you how long the test should take.
- When you are ready to start, write down the time or start the stopwatch. Or the adult helping you will tell you to begin.
- Read each question carefully and then write the answer on the answer line. Always write in full sentences, except where the question tells you otherwise. Sometimes you need to tick or underline the correct answer instead.
- Try to answer every question. If you do get stuck on a question, leave it and go on to the next one. Work quickly and try your best.
- Each test is two pages long. When you reach the end, stop. Write down the time or stop the stopwatch. Or tell the adult that you have finished.
- With the adult, work out how long you took to do the test. Fill in the **Time taken** box at the end of the test.
- The adult will mark your test and fill in the **Score** and **Target met?** boxes.
- Turn to the **Progress chart** on page 40. Write your score in the box and colour in the graph to show how many questions you got right.
- Did you get some questions wrong? You should always have another go at them before you look at the answers. Then ask the adult to check your work and help you if you are still not sure.
- Later, you will do some more of these tests. You will soon learn to work through them more quickly. The adult who is helping you will tell you what to do next.

Published by **Schofield & Sims Ltd**,
7 Mariner Court, Wakefield, West Yorkshire WF4 3FL, UK
Telephone 01484 607080
www.schofieldandsims.co.uk

This edition copyright © Schofield & Sims Ltd, 2018
First published in 2018
Third impression 2021

Author: **Siân Goodspeed**. Siân Goodspeed has asserted her moral rights under the Copyright, Designs and Patents Act, 1988, to be identified as the author of this work. Any text not otherwise attributed has been written by Siân Goodspeed and is copyright © Schofield & Sims Ltd, 2018.

Little Foxes (pages 10 and 11) are extracts from Little Foxes by Michael Morpurgo. Text copyright © 1984 Michael Morpurgo. Published by Egmont UK Ltd and used with permission. **Good Night Stories for Rebel Girls** (page 16) is an extract from Good Night Stories for Rebel Girls by Elena Favilli and Francesca Cavallo (Particular Books). Copyright © Elena Favilli and Francesca Cavallo 2017. **Five Children and It** (page 28) is an extract from Five Children and It by E. Nesbit (public domain). **From a Railway Carriage** (page 34) is an extract from A Child's Garden of Verses by Robert Louis Stevenson (public domain).

Every effort has been made to trace all copyright holders and obtain their permission to reproduce copyright material prior to publication. If notified, the publisher will rectify any errors or omissions at the earliest opportunity.

British Library Cataloguing in Publication Data. A catalogue record for this book is available from the British Library.

All rights reserved. No part of this publication may be reproduced, stored in a retrieval system, or transmitted in any form or by any means, electronic, mechanical, photocopying, recording or otherwise, without either the prior permission of the publisher or a licence permitting restricted copying in the United Kingdom issued by the Copyright Licensing Agency Ltd.

Design by **Ledgard Jepson Ltd**
Front cover design by **Ledgard Jepson Ltd**
Printed in the UK by **Page Bros (Norwich) Ltd**

ISBN 978 07217 1432 5

Comprehension

Section **1** Test **1**
continued

5. Name two things you might see at the Magical Realm.

   _____ and _____   /2

6. Name two activities you could do at the Animal Kingdom.

   _____ and _____   /2

7. According to the text, which theme park is the best place to relax at the end of the day? Why?

   _____

   _____   /2

8. Hyperbole is the use of extreme exaggeration to make a point. One example from the text has been given. Write two more examples of hyperbole from the text on the lines below.

   Example: the most exciting place on Earth!

   _____

   _____   /2

9. Why do you think the author used so much hyperbole in this brochure?

   _____

   _____   /2

10. The following passage has had some words removed. Choose the word that best fits and write it on the line. Not all the words are needed and you may use each word only once.

    | park | outdoor | sustenance | disappoint | exercise | recharge |
    | entertained | find | located | theme | occupy | holidays |

    After an action-packed day at Wonder World's **a)** _____ parks,

    where better to **b)** _____ your batteries than at the Wonder

    World Hotel. With four **c)** _____ swimming pools and a fun-filled

    kids' club, there is plenty to keep children **d)** _____ while parents chill

    out in the spa or **e)** _____ in the gym. If you're in need of some

    f) _____, try one of our family-friendly restaurants or dial up some

    room service. **g)** _____ right in the heart of the Magical Realm,

    close to all the action, this popular hotel will not **h)** _____!   /8

    | Score: | Time taken: | Target met? |

English Rapid Tests 4   5

Section 1 Test 2

Grammar and punctuation

Target time: **10 minutes**

1. Change the tense of each sentence below into the tense written in brackets. Write the new sentence on the line.

    Example: Lorna teaches in a primary school. (FUTURE)
    <u>Lorna will teach in a primary school.</u>

    a) We have travelled to many different countries. (FUTURE)

    _____

    b) Amar did his best in his history exam. (PAST PERFECT)

    _____

    c) Keira wanted to visit the science museum. (PRESENT)

    _____

    d) Sebastian is learning how to ride a motorbike. (PRESENT PERFECT)

    _____

    /4

2. The following passage has some punctuation missing. Write out the passage on the lines, adding in the correct punctuation.

    Jessica was counting down the minutes until school finished; she didnt take her eye off the clock It was their very last friday before Jessicas family went to france on holiday. She had written down her packing list sun hat lilo and goggles were still to go in her suitcase. The bell rang. School's over let's go she exclaimed

    _____

    _____

    _____

    _____

    /6

6

Schofield & Sims

Grammar and punctuation

Section **1** Test **2**
continued

3. Choose the correct pronouns from the box below to complete each sentence. Write them on the lines. You may use each word only once.

| him | us | it | she | herself | she | he | them |

Example: I love __my__ cat, Felix, because __he__ is so playful.

a) Leo's bedroom was messy, so his nan told _____ to tidy _____.

b) We were excited to see our mum when _____ picked _____ up.

c) What did _____ do with his old toys? Did he sell _____?

d) When my sister fell over, _____ was lucky not to hurt _____.

/4

4. Choose the correct word or phrase from the box below to complete each sentence. Write it on the line. You may use each word or phrase only once.

| due to | but | since | instead | although | so that |

a) The rain poured down _____ the match carried on.

b) Mum said the road was closed _____ an accident.

c) Malek went to the gym _____ he could build up his muscles.

d) Lyra said she would walk home _____ it was a very long way.

/4

5. In each of the sentences below, two of the words have swapped places. Work out which words need to be swapped for the sentence to make sense. Underline the two words.

Example: Her favourite golf was sport.

a) The nettles were overgrown with weeds and flowerbeds.

b) "swimming is it necessary that I go why?" asked the boy.

c) Jade was catching at throwing and adept, and so joined the netball team.

d) In November, a new elected was president.

/4

| Score: | | Time taken: | | Target met? | |

English Rapid Tests 4

7

Section 1 Test 3

Spelling and vocabulary

Target time: 10 minutes

1. Synonyms are words that have the same or very similar meanings. Underline the word in each set of brackets that is a synonym of the word in bold.

    Example: fast   (slow   <u>quick</u>   feet)

    a) **aggressive**   (agreeable   hostile   loud)

    b) **companion**   (enemy   comparison   friend)

    c) **affectionate**   (loving   unkind   infection)

    d) **nimble**   (nasty   agile   bite)

    /4

2. Antonyms are words that have opposite meanings. Underline the word in each set of brackets that is an antonym of the word in bold.

    Example: up   (out   <u>down</u>   through)

    a) **profit**   (win   money   loss)

    b) **comply**   (submit   compare   disobey)

    c) **energetic**   (lethargic   undone   spritely)

    d) **sturdy**   (fragile   robust   week)

    /4

3. Write out each abbreviation below in full on the line.

    Example: Dr   <u>Doctor</u>

    a) Ave.   _____

    b) mm   _____

    c) PE   _____

    d) gov.   _____

    /4

8

Schofield & Sims

Spelling and vocabulary

Section **1** Test **3**
continued

4. The passage below contains <u>six</u> spelling errors. Find each word that is spelt incorrectly, underline it, and then write the correct spelling on the line.

> On the last Friday of every month, I attend the book club at our local librery. Each month, we read and review a diferent book that a member of the club has choosen. It is a great opurtunity to share opiniuns with other like-minded people. My favourite genrer is science fiction.

_____   _____

_____   _____

_____   _____

/6

5. Sort each word in the word bank into the correct category by writing it in the table below. The first row has been done for you.

Word bank

maroon	magenta	grey	silver
fuchsia	~~cherry~~	burgundy	teal
cyan	beige	olive	~~turquoise~~
plum	amber	~~lilac~~	scarlet
~~yellow~~	crimson	jade	violet

Red/Brown	Blue/Green	Purple/Pink	Other
cherry	turquoise	lilac	yellow

/4

Score:	Time taken:	Target met?

English Rapid Tests 4

9

Section 1 Test 4

Comprehension

Target time: **10 minutes**

Read the text and answer the questions below.

Extract from **Little Foxes, by Michael Morpurgo**

Billy Bunch came in a box one wintry night ten years ago. It was a large box with these words stencilled across it: 'Handle with care. This side up. Perishable.'

For Police Constable William Fazackerly this was a night never to be forgotten. He had pounded the streets all night checking shop doors and windows, but it was too cold a night
5 even for burglars. As he came round the corner and saw the welcome blue light above the door of the Police Station, he was thinking only of the mug of sweet hot tea waiting for him in the canteen. He bounded up the steps two at a time and nearly tripped over the box at the top.

At first it looked like a box of flowers, for a great bunch of carnations – blue from the light above – filled it from end to end. He crouched down and parted the flowers. Billy lay there
10 swathed in blankets up to his chin. A fluffy woollen bonnet covered his head and ears so that all Police Constable Fazackerly could see of him were two wide open eyes and a toothless mouth that smiled cherubically up at him. There was a note attached to the flowers: 'Please look after him', it read.

Police Constable Fazackerly sat down beside the box and tickled the child's voluminous cheeks
15 and the smile broke at once into a giggle so infectious that the young policeman dissolved into a high-pitched chuckle that soon brought the Desk Sergeant and half the night shift out to investigate. The flowers – and they turned white once they were inside – were dropped unceremoniously into Police Constable Fazackerly's helmet, and the child was borne into the Station by the Desk Sergeant, a most proprietary grin creasing his face. "Don't stand there
20 gawping," he said. "I want hot water bottles, lots of 'em and quickly."

Write **A**, **B**, **C** or **D** on the answer line.

1. What was the weather like on the night the box was found?
   A hot and humid
   B damp and drizzly
   C freezing cold
   D windy and wet

   _____ /1

2. Where was the box found?
   A on the steps outside the Police Station
   B in the street
   C inside the Police Station
   D at the florist's

   _____ /1

3. What was found in the box?
   A a blue light
   B a cup of tea
   C a baby boy
   D a bunch of roses

   _____ /1

4. What was Billy wearing?
   A a nappy
   B blankets and a hat
   C pyjamas
   D a policeman's helmet

   _____ /1

Comprehension

Section **1** Test **4**
continued

5. Why was it 'a night never to be forgotten' for Constable Fazackerly?

_____

_____ /2

6. a) Where was the note found?

_____

b) What did the note say?

_____ /2

7. Why did the flowers turn white once they were inside the Police Station?

_____

_____ /2

8. The words on the left in blue can all be found in the text. Draw lines to match each word with its meaning in the text.

perishable   staring in a stupid manner

cherubically   likely to quickly spread or influence others

infectious   likely to decay or go off quickly

gawping   innocent, like a little angel   /4

9. The following passage is from later in *Little Foxes*, but it has had some words removed. Choose the word that best fits and write it on the line. Not all the words are needed and you may use each word only once.

| pensive | beautiful | hair | overshadowed | parting | length |
| charm | birthday | more | attractive | endear | offend |

By his first **a)** _____, Billy Bunch had entirely lost the smile he had

come with. A grim seriousness **b)** _____ him and he became

c) _____ and silent, and this did nothing to **d)** _____

him to the nurses who, try as they did, could find little to love in the child. Neither was he an

e) _____ boy. Once he had lost the chubby **f)** _____

of his infancy, his ears were seen to stick out **g)** _____ than they should

and they could find no **h)** _____ for his hair which would never lie down.   /8

Score: _____   Time taken: _____   Target met: _____

English Rapid Tests 4   11

Section 1 Test 5

Grammar and punctuation

Target time: 10 minutes

1. Choose the correct determiner from the box below to complete each sentence. Write it on the line. You may use each word only once.

an	many	this	my
most	every	our	all

   a) It took _____ hours to complete my project.

   b) On _____ days, my dad works until 7.00 p.m.

   c) _____ house on our street has the same front door.

   d) _____ elephants have long trunks and big ears.

   /4

2. Sort each noun in the word bank into the correct category by writing it in the table below. The first row has been done for you. You may use each word only once.

   Word bank

loyalty	~~anger~~	fish	anxiety
Thursday	England	calm	~~flock~~
flower	biscuit	~~Nathan~~	woman
~~chair~~	choir	Jupiter	Ford
fear	team	crowd	herd

Abstract noun	Collective noun	Proper noun	Other nouns
anger	flock	Nathan	chair

   /4

12   Schofield & Sims

Grammar and punctuation

Section **1** Test **5**
continued

3. Write out each phrase on the line, using an apostrophe to show possession.

   Example: the kindness of the woman   the woman's kindness

   a) the saddle belonging to the horse _____

   b) the droning of the aeroplanes _____

   c) the debut of the actress _____

   d) the cheers of the crowd _____

   e) the buttons on the dress _____

   f) the laughter of the babies _____

   /6

4. Choose the most appropriate fronted adverbial to start each sentence below. Write it on the line. You may use each phrase only once.

   | In the darkness | In a time long ago |
   | In a puff of smoke | With a sharp knife |

   a) _____, in a faraway kingdom, there lived an old wizard.

   b) _____, chop the tomatoes into small pieces.

   c) _____, the genie appeared.

   d) _____, she couldn't see a thing.

   /4

5. Punctuate the direct speech in these sentences.

   a) At the end of term announced the teacher there will be a talent show.

   b) Bruno saw a rabbit explained Alicia and he ran off after it.

   c) Use your plate said Dad or you'll get crumbs everywhere.

   d) Many years ago began the storyteller there was a giant who lived in a cave.

   /4

   Score: _____   Time taken: _____   Target met? _____

English Rapid Tests 4   13

Section 1 Test 6

Spelling and vocabulary

Target time: **10 minutes**

1. One word from the first set of brackets goes together with one word from the second set of brackets to make a new word. Underline the two words and write the new word on the line.

   Example: (<u>in</u> out about)   (<u>to</u> game of)   <u>into</u>

   a) (shake toy rattle)   (err snake bear)   _____

   b) (pole bar long)   (gain up smooth)   _____

   c) (is on in)   (dance form stand)   _____

   d) (vine stem root)   (yard lot out)   _____

   /4

2. In each sentence below, there is an incorrectly spelt word. Find the word, underline it and then write the correct spelling on the line.

   Example: I <u>comunicate</u> with my cousin by email.   <u>communicate</u>

   a) The averige temperature in London is highest in July and August. _____

   b) It was a priviledge and honour to work alongside you. _____

   c) His relatives felt fortunate that they were so prosperus. _____

   d) I won a dictionery in the spelling tournament. _____

   /4

3. Draw lines to match each word with its definition.

   fatigue   a small part of something

   roam   not showing respect for another person

   impudent   extreme tiredness

   fragment   to wander about aimlessly

   /4

Spelling and vocabulary

Section **1** Test **6**
continued

4. Write out the words in each row on the line so that they are in alphabetical order.

Example: ring ran run ruin race   race ran ring ruin run

a) boat brick bone brine book

_____

b) hand hind hook hall hymn

_____

c) seem seam seat seal seen

_____

d) jelly jewel jolly jealous jewellery

_____

/4

5. Decide which of the homophones in bold is the correct word for each sentence. Underline the word.

Example: They saw a **heard / herd** of cows in the field.

a) It is important not to **waste / waist** water.

b) The young princess was **heir / air** to the throne.

c) They were very surprised to see a wild **boar / bore** on their trek!

d) The thief tried to **steel / steal** my neighbour's car.

e) The soldier reported to the **colonel / kernel** for further instruction.

f) The car stuck in the snow had to be **toed / towed** away.

/6

Score:	Time taken:	Target met?

English Rapid Tests 4
15

Section 2 Test 1

Comprehension

Target time: 10 minutes

Read the text and answer the questions below.

Extract from **Good Night Stories for Rebel Girls**, by Elena Favilli and Francesca Cavallo

ASHLEY FIOLEK – MOTOCROSS RACER

A little girl called Ashley was playing in the kitchen when some pans fell off the table with a massive crash. Ashley didn't even turn around. Her mom and dad decided to get her hearing tested. When the results came back, they found out that their daughter was deaf.

They learned sign language and sent Ashley to camp with other deaf kids so she could learn from them and build up her self-confidence.

Ashley's father and her grandfather loved motorcycles, so they gave her a peewee motorbike when she was three. The three of them would head to the woods, each of them on their own motorcycle. Ashley loved these outings and she started dreaming about becoming a motocross racer.

Most people told her it would be impossible. "Hearing is really important in motocross," they said. "The sound of the engine tells you when to shift gears. You have to be able to hear where the other riders are."

But Ashley could feel from the engine's vibration when to change gears. She looked for shadows in the corner of her eye and knew when someone was getting close.

In five years she won four national titles. She fell, many times! Ashley broke her left arm, her right wrist, her right ankle, her collarbone (three times) and her two front teeth, but she always recovered and got back on her bike.

Ashley has a pickup truck parked in her driveway. On the back, a bumper sticker reads: 'Honk all you want, I'm deaf!'

Write **A**, **B**, **C** or **D** on the answer line.

1. What did Ashley's parents discover when she was very young?
   A that she was deaf
   B that she was blind
   C that she was scared of heights
   D that she had learned sign language

   _____ /1

2. Who were Ashley's main influences?
   A her friends
   B her father and grandfather
   C her mother and father
   D her fans

   _____ /1

3. What was Ashley's childhood dream?
   A to learn sign language
   B to ride BMX bikes
   C to be a motocross racer
   D to be a stunt rider

   _____ /1

4. Which of the following did Ashley not break?
   A her ankle
   B her wrist
   C her collarbone
   D her jaw

   _____ /1

Comprehension

Section **2** Test **1**
continued

5. What happened to make Ashley's parents think that she might be deaf?

_____

_____ /2

6. Which <u>two</u> actions did Ashley's parents take after they found out she was deaf?

_____

_____ /2

7. Why did people say Ashley's deafness would make it impossible for her to do motocross?

_____

_____ /2

8. How did Ashley use her other senses to overcome the fact that she could not hear when racing?

_____

_____ /2

9. Which <u>two</u> adjectives best describe Ashley's personality? Tick the boxes.

timid ☐   bold ☐   arrogant ☐   determined ☐   cautious ☐   /2

10. The following passage is an information text about motocross, but it has had some words removed. Choose the word that best fits and write it on the line. Not all the words are needed and you may use each word only once.

| reached | racing | international | crash | originated |
| popularity | thriving | available | circuits | flourish |

Motocross is a type of motorcycle **a)** _____ held on enclosed off-road

b) _____. The sport **c)** _____ in the UK in the early

1900s. It grew in **d)** _____, and over time clubs and competitions were

established all over Britain. In the 1970s, the sport began to **e)** _____

in the United States as well. This made for exciting racing, as **f)** _____

rivalries developed. Today, motocross is still a **g)** _____ sport, with big

sponsorship deals and prize money **h)** _____ for the best riders.   /8

Score: _____   Time taken: _____   Target met? _____

English Rapid Tests 4   17

Section 2 Test 2

Grammar and punctuation

Target time: **10 minutes**

1. Write the missing words in the table. The first row has been done for you.

Adjective	Comparative	Superlative
big	bigger	biggest
good		
cheap		
expensive		
lovely		

/4

2. Read the sentences below. In each sentence, underline the verb form that is in the past perfect.

   Example: Once Suki <u>had learnt</u> to ride a bike, there was no stopping her!

   a) As soon as Nadia had finished one book, she started another.

   b) The fairy had warned the children not to enter the forest, but to no avail.

   c) Sue had shut the shop in time for dinner.

   d) By the time my mum had mowed the lawn, it was almost dark.

/4

3. Write **it's** or **its** on each line below so that the sentences make sense.

   Example: My school is holding <u>its</u> annual firework display on Saturday.

   a) _____ a long way home.

   b) Ruby's hamster nibbles _____ cage.

   c) Logan thought the museum shut _____ doors at 4.00 p.m.

   d) I think _____ time to sleep now.

/4

18

Schofield & Sims

Grammar and punctuation

Section 2 Test 2 continued

4. Sort each word in the word bank into the correct word class by writing it in the table below. You may use each word only once. The first row has been done for you.

Word bank

behind	dance	~~under~~	kindly
sincerely	humorous	scream	react
~~run~~	into	ancient	~~small~~
lively	delicate	endure	after
foolishly	~~slowly~~	until	energetically

Preposition	Verb	Adjective	Adverb
under	run	small	slowly

/4

5. In each of the sentences below, <u>two</u> of the words have swapped places. Work out which words need to be swapped for the sentence to make sense. Underline the two words.

Example: Her favourite <u>golf</u> was <u>sport</u>.

a) Dolphins intelligent very are sea creatures.

b) The storm night relentlessly throughout the raged.

c) Lucy felt the when she heard disappointed result of the election.

d) The children were delighted to it discover had snowed overnight.

e) Although they were years, they hadn't spoken for many sisters.

f) The pupil's could not abide the teacher lateness.

/6

Score: Time taken: Target met?

English Rapid Tests 4

19

Section 2 Test 3

Spelling and vocabulary

Target time: **10 minutes**

1. Two of the words in each set do not go with the other three. Underline these <u>two</u> words.

   Example: dark <u>bright</u> gloomy <u>light</u> dusky

   a) zealous   nonchalant   ardent   fervent   bored

   b) liver   spine   intestine   skull   kidney

   c) obstacle   benefit   complication   hindrance   convenience

   d) angry   vigilant   irate   attentive   watchful

   /4

2. Decide which of the homophones in bold is the correct word for each sentence. Underline the word.

   Example: They saw a **heard / <u>herd</u>** of cows in the field.

   a) Salma really wanted to reach the **peak / peek** of the mountain.

   b) The little boy got lost in the meat **isle / aisle** of the supermarket.

   c) Holly was still **morning / mourning** the loss of her pet rat.

   d) Eli's dad tried to **rows / rouse** him, but with little success.

   /4

3. Underline the word in each set of brackets that is an antonym (opposite) of the word in bold.

   Example: up   (out <u>down</u> through)

   a) **inane**   (dull   intelligent   engage)

   b) **peril**   (trapped   danger   safety)

   c) **surplus**   (lack   plenty   excess)

   d) **squalor**   (dirty   luxury   peace)

   /4

20   Schofield & Sims

English Rapid Tests 4 Answers

Notes for parents, tutors, teachers and other adult helpers

- **English Rapid Tests 4** is designed for nine- and ten-year-olds, but may also be suitable for some children of other ages.

- Remove this pull-out section before giving the book to the child.

- Before the child begins work on the first test, together read the instructions headed **What to do** on page 2. As you do so, point out to the child the suggested **Target time** for completing the test.

- Make sure the child has all the equipment in the list headed **What you need** on page 2.

- There are three sections in this book. Each section contains two comprehension tests, two grammar and punctuation tests, and two spelling and vocabulary tests.

- Explain to the child how he or she should go about timing the test. Alternatively, you may wish to time the test yourself. When the child has finished the test, together work out the **Time taken** and complete the box that appears at the end of the test.

- Mark the child's work using this pull-out section. Each test is out of 22 marks and each correct answer is worth one mark unless otherwise stated in the answers. Then complete the **Score** box at the end of the test.

- For all spelling questions, the answer must be spelt correctly for the full mark to be awarded. Where applicable, answers need to be written in full sentences and correct grammar used for marks to be awarded.

- This table shows you how to mark the **Target met?** box and the **Action** notes help you to plan the next step. However, these are suggestions only. Please use your own judgement as you decide how best to proceed.

Score	Time taken	Target met?	Action
$1-11\frac{1}{2}$	Any	Not yet	Give the child the previous book in the series. Provide help and support as needed.
$12-17\frac{1}{2}$	Any	Not yet	Encourage the child to keep practising using the tests in this book. The child may need to repeat some tests. If so, wait a few weeks or the child may simply remember the correct answers. Provide help and support as needed.
18–22	Over target – child took too long	Not yet	
18–22	On target – child took suggested time or less	Yes	Encourage the child to keep practising using further tests in this book, and to move on to the next book when you think this is appropriate.

- After finishing each test, the child should fill in the **Progress chart** on page 40.

- Whatever the test score, always encourage the child to have another go at the questions that he or she got wrong – without looking at the answers. If the child's answers are still incorrect, work through these questions together. Demonstrate the correct technique if necessary.

- If the child struggles with particular question types or areas, help him or her to develop the skills and strategies needed.

Answers

Section 1 Test 1 (pages 4–5)

1. A
2. C
3. D
4. B
5. the Wonder World Castle or fireworks or parades or Wonder World characters
   Award 1 mark for each of the above. (Maximum 2 marks.)
6. rides or shows or animal encounters/safari (or get close to the animals)
   Award 1 mark for each of the above. (Maximum 2 marks.)
7. Splash and Slide, because you can relax next to the (infinity) pool or because you can relax on the water (on a giant lilo).
   Award 1 mark for naming Splash and Slide, and 1 mark for giving either of the reasons above.
8. set your imagination on fire; you'll be blown away; bursting with the planet's most magical characters; dreams come true; fairytales become a reality; awe-inspiring/heart-stopping rides; breathtaking animal encounters; lose yourself in the magic of cinema; blows all other water parks out of the water
   Award 1 mark for each of the above. (Maximum 2 marks.)
9. The author has used hyperbole to give the brochure more impact or to make the theme parks sound exciting in order to encourage people to visit them.
   Award 1 mark for referring to creating excitement in the reader, and 1 mark for explaining that this will lead to more visitors.
10. a) theme
    b) recharge
    c) outdoor
    d) entertained
    e) exercise
    f) sustenance
    g) Located
    h) disappoint

Section 1 Test 2 (pages 6–7)

1. a) We will travel to many different countries.
   b) Amar had done his best in his history exam.
   c) Keira wants to visit the science museum.
   d) Sebastian has learnt/learned how to ride a motorbike.
   This question is testing the child's understanding of tense and verb–subject agreement. In part a, 'We are going to travel to many different countries.' is also acceptable.

2. Jessica was counting down the minutes until school finished; she didn't take her eye off the clock**.** It was their very last **F**riday before Jessica's family went to **F**rance on holiday. She had written down her packing list**:** sun hat**,** lilo and goggles were still to go in her suitcase. The bell rang. **"**School's over **–** let's go**!"** she exclaimed**.**
   This question is testing the child's ability to make sense of a passage that is missing punctuation marks and to insert the punctuation correctly where needed. The parts in bold show where punctuation has been corrected. A semicolon instead of a dash is also acceptable. Award half a mark for each correct item of punctuation inserted. (Maximum 6 marks.)

3. a) him, it
   b) she, us
   c) he, them
   d) she, herself
   This question is testing the child's understanding of the correct use of pronouns. Award half a mark for each correct word.

4. a) but
   b) due to
   c) so that
   d) although
   This question is testing the child's understanding of how co-ordinating and subordinating conjunctions link ideas in a sentence.

A2   Schofield & Sims

Answers

5. a) nettles, flowerbeds
    b) swimming, why
    c) catching, adept
    d) elected, president

    This question is testing the child's knowledge of correct word order. Both correct words must be underlined in order for the mark to be awarded.

Section 1 Test 3 (pages 8–9)

1. a) hostile
    b) friend
    c) loving
    d) agile

    This question is testing the child's knowledge of synonyms.

2. a) loss
    b) disobey
    c) lethargic
    d) fragile

    This question is testing the child's knowledge of antonyms.

3. a) Avenue
    b) millimetre
    c) Physical Education
    d) government

4. library, different, chosen, opportunity, opinions, genre

    Award 1 mark for each correct answer. Award only half a mark if the error has been underlined but not corrected accurately. Each correct spelling can be written on any of the answer lines for the mark to be awarded.

5.
Red/ Brown	Blue/ Green	Purple/ Pink	Other
cherry	turquoise	lilac	yellow
crimson	teal	plum	silver
scarlet	cyan	violet	grey
maroon	jade	magenta	beige
burgundy	olive	fuchsia	amber

This question is testing the child's ability to assign words to different categories. Award 1 mark for 4–7 correct words; 2 marks for 8–11 correct words; 3 marks for 12–15 correct words and 4 marks for 16 correct words. (Maximum 4 marks.)

Section 1 Test 4 (pages 10–11)

1. C
2. A
3. C
4. B
5. He found a baby in a box and that is something you would remember forever.

    Award 1 mark for references to the baby, and 1 mark for references to the fact that this event was unusual or unforgettable.

6. a) The note was found in the baby's box. or The note was found attached to the flowers.
    b) The note said to look after the baby. or 'Please look after him.'

    Award 1 mark for each correct question part.

7. The flowers were actually white but they had appeared blue as they were under the blue light outside the Police Station.

    Award 1 mark for referring to the fact that the flowers were actually white, and 1 mark for referring to the fact that it was the blue light outside making them appear blue.

8.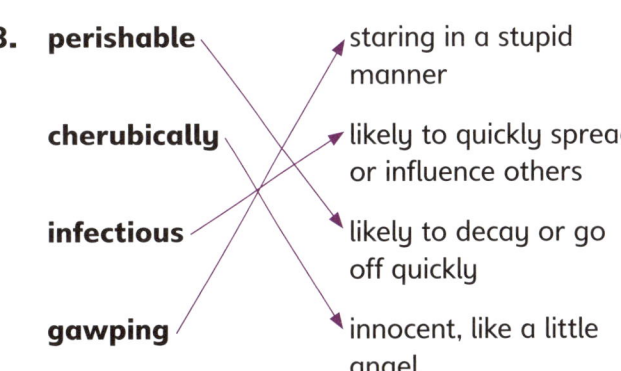

English Rapid Tests 4 Answers

Answers

Section 1 Test 4 (pages 10–11) continued

9.
a) birthday
b) overshadowed
c) pensive
d) endear
e) attractive
f) charm
g) more
h) parting

Section 1 Test 5 (pages 12–13)

1.
a) many
b) most
c) Every
d) All

This question is testing the child's ability to use determiners correctly.

2.

Abstract noun	Collective noun	Proper noun	Other nouns
anger	flock	Nathan	chair
fear	crowd	Jupiter	fish
calm	herd	Ford	woman
anxiety	choir	Thursday	flower
loyalty	team	England	biscuit

This question is testing the child's ability to assign words to different word classes. Award 1 mark for 4–7 correct words; 2 marks for 8–11 correct words; 3 marks for 12–15 correct words and 4 marks for 16 correct words. (Maximum 4 marks.)

3.
a) the horse's saddle
b) the aeroplanes' droning
c) the actress's debut (or the actress' debut)
d) the crowd's cheers
e) the dress's buttons (or the dress' buttons)
f) the babies' laughter

This question is testing the child's ability to use apostrophes to show possession.

4.
a) In a time long ago
b) With a sharp knife
c) In a puff of smoke
d) In the darkness

This question is testing the child's ability to select appropriate fronted adverbial phrases.

5.
a) "At the end of term," announced the teacher, "there will be a talent show."
b) "Bruno saw a rabbit," explained Alicia, "and he ran off after it."
c) "Use your plate," said Dad, "or you'll get crumbs everywhere."
d) "Many years ago," began the storyteller, "there was a giant who lived in a cave."

This question is testing the child's ability to use speech marks to show direct speech.

Section 1 Test 6 (pages 14–15)

1.
a) rattlesnake
b) bargain
c) inform
d) vineyard

This question is testing the child's ability to put two words together to make a new word.

2.
a) average
b) privilege
c) prosperous
d) dictionary

This question is testing the child's ability to identify and correct spelling errors.

3.

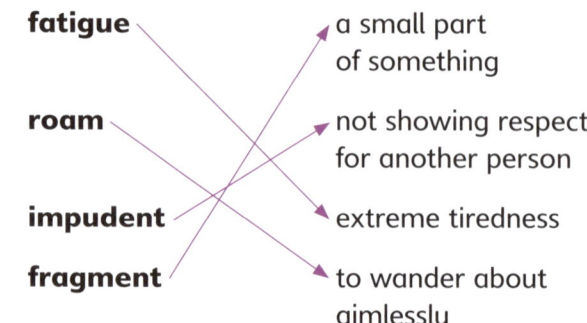

fatigue — extreme tiredness
roam — to wander about aimlessly
impudent — not showing respect for another person
fragment — a small part of something

This question is testing the child's knowledge of word meanings.

A4

Schofield & Sims

Answers

4. **a)** boat   bone   book   brick   brine
   b) hall   hand   hind   hook   hymn
   c) seal   seam   seat   seem   seen
   d) jealous   jelly   jewel   jewellery   jolly

   This question is testing the child's knowledge of alphabetical order.

5. **a)** waste
   b) heir
   c) boar
   d) steal
   e) colonel
   f) towed

   This question is testing the child's ability to distinguish between common homophones.

Section 2 Test 1 (pages 16–17)

1. A
2. B
3. C
4. D
5. Ashley did not react to the loud noise when a pile of pans fell on the floor in the kitchen.

   Award 1 mark for references to the pans falling on the floor, and 1 mark for references to the fact that she did not react to the noise.

6. They learnt sign language and they sent Ashley to a camp for deaf children.

   Award 1 mark for references to her parents learning sign language, and 1 mark for references to them sending her to a camp for deaf children.

7. They said that she needed to hear the sound of the engine to know when to change gears and she needed to hear where the other riders were.

   Award 1 mark for references to her needing to hear the sound of the engine for changing gears, and 1 mark for references to her needing to hear where the other riders were.

8. Ashley could feel from the engine's vibration when to change gear and she could work out where the other riders were by seeing their shadows in the corners of her eyes.

   Award 1 mark for references to the fact that she could feel the engine's vibration, and 1 mark for references to the fact that she could see the other riders' shadows in the corners of her eyes.

9. bold and determined

   Award 1 mark for each correctly ticked box. If more than two boxes are ticked, deduct 1 mark for every extra box ticked.

10. **a)** racing
    b) circuits
    c) originated
    d) popularity
    e) flourish
    f) international
    g) thriving
    h) available

Section 2 Test 2 (pages 18–19)

1.

Adjective	Comparative	Superlative
big	bigger	biggest
good	better	best
cheap	cheaper	cheapest
expensive	more expensive	most expensive
lovely	lovelier	loveliest

This question is testing the child's understanding of comparative and superlative adjectives. Award half a mark for each correctly spelt word/phrase. (Maximum 4 marks.)

2. **a)** had finished
   b) had warned
   c) had shut
   d) had mowed

   This question is testing the child's understanding of the past perfect tense.

Answers

Section 2 Test 2 (pages 18–19) continued

3. a) It's
   b) its
   c) its
   d) it's

   This question is testing the child's understanding of the difference between the possessive determiner 'its' and the contraction 'it's' (it is).

4.

Preposition	Verb	Adjective	Adverb
under	run	small	slowly
behind	dance	ancient	kindly
into	scream	delicate	sincerely
after	react	lively	foolishly
until	endure	humorous	energetically

   This question is testing the child's ability to assign words to different word classes. Award 1 mark for 4–7 correct words; 2 marks for 8–11 correct words; 3 marks for 12–15 correct words and 4 marks for 16 correct words. (Maximum 4 marks.) Note that 'behind' and 'after' can also be adverbs, and 'kindly' can also be an adjective, but the answer given is the only way in which the table can be completed using each word only once.

5. a) intelligent, are
   b) night, raged
   c) the, disappointed
   d) it, discover
   e) years, sisters
   f) pupil's, teacher

   This question is testing the child's knowledge of correct word order. Both correct words must be underlined in order for the mark to be awarded.

Section 2 Test 3 (pages 20–21)

1. a) nonchalant, bored (all the others are synonyms for 'zealous')
   b) spine, skull (all the others are internal organs)
   c) benefit, convenience (all the others are synonyms for 'impediment')
   d) angry, irate (all the others are synonyms for 'vigilant')

   This question is testing the child's vocabulary and their ability to identify common features of words in order to find the link.

2. a) peak
   b) aisle
   c) mourning
   d) rouse

   This question is testing the child's ability to distinguish between common homophones.

3. a) intelligent
   b) safety
   c) lack
   d) luxury

   This question is testing the child's knowledge of antonyms.

4. a) who's
   b) shan't
   c) I've
   d) let's
   e) they're
   f) she'd

   This question is testing the child's ability to spell contractions correctly. The word must be spelt correctly with the apostrophe in the right place in order for the mark to be awarded.

5. a) E, military
   b) C, professor
   c) no error
   d) B, permission

   This question is testing the child's ability to proofread and spell words. Award 1 mark for each correct question part. Award only half a mark if the error is correctly identified but the child's spelling is incorrect.

Answers

Section 2 Test 4 (pages 22–23)

1. C
2. B
3. B
4. D
5. A person screams because they are afraid of spiders or because the spider makes them jump.
   Award 1 mark for references to a person/human/man/woman/boy/girl, and 1 mark for references to them either being afraid of spiders or surprised by the spider.
6. The spider freezes because she is startled by the sound of the scream and she is not sure what to do/is not able to think clearly/is confused/pauses to think about where to go next.
   Award 1 mark for references to the fact that the noise or scream startles or surprises her, and 1 mark for references to the fact that she stops moving as she is confused/cannot think straight/is considering where to go. Answers suggesting that she freezes so that she is not seen or to avoid danger/to think about where is the safest place to go are also acceptable.
7. gliding or darting or scurrying or propels or hurtling
   Award half a mark for each word. (Maximum 2 marks.)
8. The spider is such a small creature that she does not understand why something as large as a human would be scared of her.
   Award 1 mark for references to the spider being confused, and 1 mark for references to the reason for this being that she scared a person or that she finds the world daunting.
9. The spider is an 'explorer' because she is travelling around the room, and she is 'unwelcome' because the other occupant of the room is not happy that she is there.
   Award 1 mark for references to the fact that the spider is like an explorer because she is travelling around the room/discovering new places, and 1 mark for references to the fact that the person in the room is not happy that she is there/does not like spiders/was shocked to see her.

10.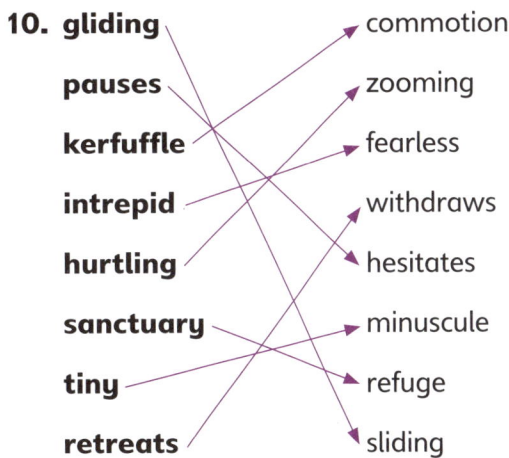
    gliding — commotion
    pauses — zooming
    kerfuffle — fearless
    intrepid — withdraws
    hurtling — hesitates
    sanctuary — minuscule
    tiny — refuge
    retreats — sliding

Section 2 Test 5 (pages 24–25)

1. a) has or had
   b) will
   c) are
   d) were or are
   e) do or would
   f) have
   This question is testing the child's ability to identify the correct auxiliary verbs, paying attention to verb–subject and tense agreement.

2. a) The cake**,** which was very sticky**,** tasted delicious.
   b) Lila's brother**,** who goes to university**,** will be home for the summer.
   c) The theme park **–** which had more than 30 rides **–** was an exciting day out.
   d) She put all her PE kit **–** trainers, T-shirt and shorts **–** into her bag.
   This question is testing the child's ability to use dashes or commas to show parenthesis. Commas or dashes could be used in each sentence, although dashes tend to be used in more formal texts. In part **d**, the sentence already contains a comma due to the list of items, so dashes work better.

English Rapid Tests 4 Answers

A7

Answers

Section 2 Test 5 (pages 24–25) continued

3. a) the girl's plane
    b) the bees' buzzing
    c) the children's happiness
    d) Carlos's (or Carlos') hat

    This question is testing the child's ability to use apostrophes to show possession.

4. a) his
    b) hers
    c) mine
    d) ours

    This question is testing the child's ability to identify the correct possessive pronoun ('his', 'hers', 'mine' and 'ours').

5. a) **re**juvenated
    b) **inter**jected
    c) **auto**biographies
    d) **super**human

    This question is testing the child's ability to identify the correct prefixes from **re–**, **inter–**, **auto–** and **super–**.

Section 2 Test 6 (pages 26–27)

1. a) crave
    b) pretend
    c) ostentatious
    d) passive
    e) torching
    f) various

    This question is testing the child's knowledge of synonyms.

2. a) gem (all the others are items of jewellery)
    b) swings (all the others are public events)
    c) quadrilateral (all the others are types of triangle)
    d) platypus (all the others are types of bird)

    This question is testing the child's vocabulary and their ability to identify common features of words in order to find the odd one out.

3. a) date of birth
    b) department
    c) for example
    d) October

4. a) carpet
    b) postage
    c) door
    d) tearing

    This question is testing the child's ability to spot how two words can go together to make a new word, and their awareness of how the letter sounds may change when the words are put together.

5. a) E, confidential
    b) E, mischievous
    c) no error
    d) C, recommended

    This question is testing the child's ability to proofread and spell words. Award only half a mark if the error is correctly identified but the child's spelling is incorrect.

Section 3 Test 1 (pages 28–29)

1. B
2. C
3. B
4. A
5. surprised, curious, excited, confused (or similar)

    Award 1 mark for each correct word. (Maximum 2 marks.) Do not award a mark for any word that suggests the children are afraid as there is no indication of this in the text.

6. a) a Psammead
    b) a Sand-fairy

    Award 1 mark for each correct question part. Do not award a mark if the child writes 'a Sammyadd' for part **a** as that is not the word that the creature uses.

Answers

7. The creature seemed surprised because it thought that everyone should know what a Sand-fairy was. This may be because Sand-fairies used to be highly regarded or there were a lot of them.

   Award 2 marks for references to the fact that the creature thought everyone should know what a Sand-fairy is. Award a further 2 marks if the child provides a reasonable suggestion as to why that might be.

8. gentle, kind, thoughtful, considerate, polite (or similar)

   Award 1 mark for each correct word. (Maximum 2 marks.)

9. No, I don't think Jane knew what a Sand-fairy was even though she says that she recognises it now. She said this because the Sand-fairy was getting upset and she did not want to hurt its feelings.

   This question is testing whether the child understands that Jane is lying when she says "Of course I see you are, now. It's quite plain now one comes to look at you." in lines 21–22. Award 2 marks if the child understands that Jane did not recognise the creature to be a Sand-fairy despite what she says. Award a further 2 marks if the child gives a reasonable explanation for why Jane might have acted in this way.

10. The Sand-fairy seemed 'less disagreeable' because Robert said it was the 'wonderfullest thing' he had ever seen. This flattered the Sand-fairy and made it feel better about the fact that the children had not known what it was.

    Award 2 marks for an answer showing an understanding that Robert is complimenting the Sand-fairy, and 2 marks for an answer showing an understanding that the Sand-fairy is flattered by Robert's comments.

Section 3 Test 2 (pages 30–31)

1. a) "Remember your glasses!" her mother shouted after her.
   b) She had chosen a title for her novel: 'The True Story of Louisa'.
   c) "Whose pen is this?" asked Beth. "It's Lauren's," replied Callum.
   d) "Don't let me forget," James said. "The appointment's at 5.00 p.m. today."

   This question is testing the child's ability to spot missing punctuation marks. Parts **a** and **c** test understanding of speech marks. Part **b** tests capitalisation of the first letter in a sentence and usage of colons. Part **d** tests usage of apostrophes in contractions. In part **b**, a dash instead of a colon is also acceptable. Award half a mark for each error corrected. (Maximum 4 marks.)

2. a) teach (The transition to secondary school was turbulent for Molly.)
   b) old (They took the toddlers to the park and played all afternoon.)
   c) garden ("Will you behave impeccably today?" asked their mother.)
   d) ever (Leela's ambition was to become a radio show host.)
   e) beef (They went to the pub for lunch so that nobody had to wash up.)
   f) vegetable (Mushrooms and chicken are my favourite pizza toppings.)

   This question is testing the child's knowledge of correct word order.

3. a) (proper) noun, determiner
   b) adverb, adjective
   c) adverb, adjective
   d) adjective, preposition

   This question is testing the child's ability to identify the correct word class. Award half a mark for each correct word class.

4. a) strengthen
   b) dramatise
   c) solidify
   d) activate

   This question is testing the child's ability to recognise verbs with the suffixes **–en**, **–ise**, **–ify** and **–ate**.

English Rapid Tests 4 Answers

Answers

Section 3 Test 2 (pages 30–31) continued

5.
a) Ravi asked Mrs Grant **(**his next-door neighbour**)** if she would sponsor him.
b) Archie's cats **(**Jessie and Alf**)** are very friendly.
c) My cousin **(**who is two years older than me**)** is coming to stay next week.
d) Mason's mum **(**who tends to worry a lot**)** told him not to be late home.

This question is testing the child's ability to use brackets correctly. You could explain that brackets add extra information that is not essential to the meaning of the sentence.

Section 3 Test 3 (pages 32–33)

1.
a) workforce
b) woodwork
c) worktop
d) homework

This question is testing the child's knowledge of compound words.

2.
a) penguin, ostrich (all the others are mammals)
b) October, March (all the other months begin with 'J')
c) lilac, maroon (all the others are shades of blue)
d) boar, ram (all the others are female animals)

This question is testing the child's vocabulary and their ability to identify common features of words in order to find the link.

3.
a) uncharacteristic
b) inconvenient
c) irrational
d) atypical or untypical

This question is testing the child's ability to form antonyms by adding appropriate prefixes.

4.
a) E, mischief
b) B, foreign
c) no error
d) C, relieved

This question is testing the child's ability to proofread and spell words. Award 1 mark for each correct question part. Award only half a mark if the error is correctly identified but the spelling is incorrect.

5.

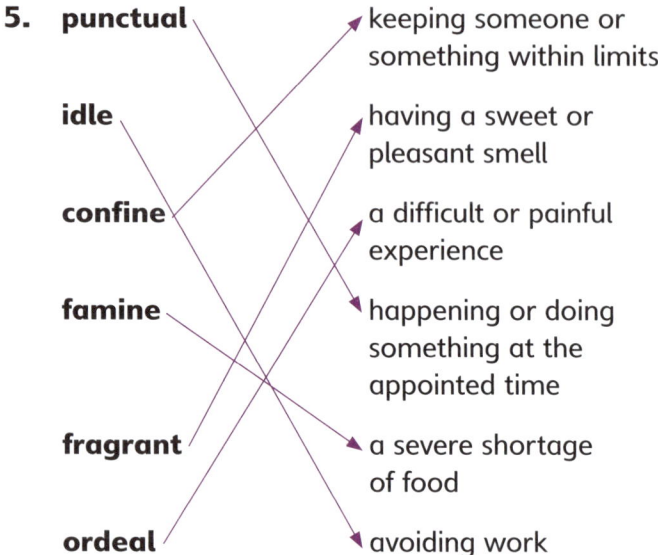

This question is testing the child's knowledge of word meanings.

Section 3 Test 4 (pages 34–35)

1. B
2. C
3. A
4. B
5. The green is an area of grass where daisies might grow so you could make daisy chains.

Award 1 mark for references to the fact that the green is an area of grass, and 1 mark for references to making daisy chains.

6. a mill and a river

7. The rhythm of the poem is very repetitive and fast, which makes you think of the movement of a train.

Award 1 mark for an appropriate comment on the rhythm of the poem, and 1 mark for answers relating the rhythm to the movement of a train.

Answers

8. Everything seen from the train is seen only for a moment before it passes out of sight.

   Award 1 mark for references to the fact that everything seen from the train is seen only briefly, and 1 mark for references to the fact that this is because of the movement of the train/everything then moves out of sight.

9. charging along like troops in a battle and fly as thick as driving rain

   Award 2 marks for each simile.

10. a) t**ypi**cally
    b) carr**iag**es
    c) en**gin**eer
    d) tra**nsp**ort
    e) elect**ric**ity
    f) envi**ron**ments

Section 3 Test 5 (pages 36–37)

1. a) She could only play at weekends.
   b) There were sheep, goats, pigs and dogs on the farm.
   c) Sadiq enquired, "Would you like some cake?"
   d) Her shopping list read: tomatoes, red onions and cheese.
   e) My friend Annie (whom I have known since birth) is coming to stay.
   f) The car engine revved loudly, she pulled out of the space, and they were off!

   This question is testing the child's ability to spot incorrect punctuation and insert correct punctuation. Part **a** tests understanding of commas and capitalisation. Part **b** tests understanding of commas. Part **c** tests punctuating direct speech and question marks. Part **d** tests usage of colons and commas. Part **e** tests usage of brackets. Part **f** tests usage of commas and capitalisation. Award half a mark for each error corrected. (Maximum 6 marks.)

2. a) did
   b) were
   c) those
   d) healthily

This question is testing the child's ability to correctly identify Standard English forms.

3. a) simple or simpler or simplest (adjective), or simplification or simplicity (abstract noun)
   b) sympathy (abstract noun) or sympathetic (adjective)
   c) beautiful (adjective) or beauty (abstract noun)
   d) short or shorter or shortest (adjective), or shortness (noun)

   This question is testing the child's ability to change the suffix of a word to change its meaning. It is also testing their ability to identify the correct word class. For each question part, award half a mark for a correct word, which must be spelt correctly, and half a mark for the correct word class.

4. a) goggles (The pool was freezing so we didn't swim for long.)
   b) tree (Grace shouted, "Wait for me!" as they ran through the field.)
   c) science (Is it true that the Earth is moving further from the Sun?)
   d) melt (My favourite flavour of ice cream is chocolate chip.)

   This question is testing the child's knowledge of correct word order.

5. a) return or upturn or downturn or overturn
   b) discount or recount or miscount
   c) mislead
   d) antibody or anybody or somebody or nobody or everybody

   This question is testing the child's ability to add a prefix to change a word's meaning.

Section 3 Test 6 (pages 38–39)

1. a) inconceivable, unthinkable
   b) ailment, illness
   c) incision, cut
   d) jeopardise, endanger

   This question is testing the child's knowledge of synonyms.

Answers

Section 3 Test 6 (pages 38–39) continued

2. a) stationary
   b) idol
   c) brewed
   d) compliments

   This question is testing the child's ability to distinguish between common homophones.

3. a) enthusiasm, indifference
   b) truthful, dishonest
   c) foe, friend
   d) obey, defy

   This question is testing the child's knowledge of antonyms.

4. a) laugh laughter life loose lose
   b) terrible terrify trailer train transistor
   c) under unexpected until unto unusual
   d) zeal zealot zealous zebra zero

   This question is testing the child's knowledge of alphabetical order.

5. a) e**qua**tor
   b) illeg**ible**
   c) inter**vie**w
   d) interna**tio**nal
   e) c**ir**culation
   f) c**ent**ipede

Spelling and vocabulary Section **2** Test **3** continued

4. Write out the following words as a contraction on the line. Remember your apostrophes!

   Example: do not   don't

   a) who is   _____

   b) shall not   _____

   c) I have   _____

   d) let us   _____

   e) they are   _____

   f) she had   _____

   /6

5. Some of the following sentences contain a spelling error. If you spot an error, circle the letter above it and write the correct spelling on the line. If there is no error, write **no error** on the line.

a)

A	B	C	D	E
My mum	spent her	working life	in the	militery.

_____

b)

A	B	C	D	E
My uncle	is a	proffesor of	ancient	history.

_____

c)

A	B	C	D	E
The soldiers	conducted a	thorough	search of	the vehicle.

_____

d)

A	B	C	D	E
Please sign	the permision	slip for	my school	photograph.

_____

/4

Score: _____   Time taken: _____   Target met? _____

English Rapid Tests 4

Section 2 Test 4

Comprehension

Target time: **10 minutes**

Read the text and answer the questions below.

The Unwelcome Explorer, by Siân Goodspeed

Silent but fast on a hand-spun zip wire,
Gliding down from the ceiling she lands by the fire.
She pauses to check that no danger's in sight,
Then propels herself forwards with all of her might.

5 Darting and scurrying, so daring and brave,
Seeking refuge under the cushiony cave.
A shriek, a kerfuffle, an ear-splitting scream,
It appears her adventure has not gone unseen.

For a moment, she freezes, surprised by the din.
10 It's hard to think clearly when panic sets in.
Takes a deep breath, her goal within sight,
The intrepid explorer once more takes flight.

Hurtling onwards, into sanctuary, dark,
This tiny adventurer's leaving her mark.
15 Retreats under cover for safety's sake,
Bemused at the terror she's left in her wake.

Write **A**, **B**, **C** or **D** on the answer line.

1. Who is the 'intrepid explorer' in the poem?
   - **A** a rat
   - **B** a girl
   - **C** a spider
   - **D** a boy

   _____ /1

2. What is the 'hand-spun zip wire'?
   - **A** a fun ride
   - **B** the spider's web
   - **C** a rope
   - **D** the rat's tail

   _____ /1

3. What is the rhyming pattern of the poem?
   - **A** ABAB
   - **B** AABB
   - **C** ABCB
   - **D** AAAB

   _____ /1

4. Where does the explorer go to seek safety?
   - **A** the fire
   - **B** a cave
   - **C** a den
   - **D** under the sofa

   _____ /1

Comprehension

Section **2** Test **4**
continued

5. In line 7, who or what do you think makes the 'ear-splitting scream'? Why do they scream?

_____

_____ /2

6. In line 9, why does the explorer freeze?

_____

_____ /2

7. List <u>four</u> verbs that the poet uses to create the feeling of fast movement in the poem.

_____   _____

_____   _____ /2

8. Read the last line of the poem. Explain in your own words what this means.

_____

_____ /2

9. Why do you think the poem is entitled 'The Unwelcome Explorer'?

_____

_____ /2

10. The words on the left in blue can all be found in the text. Draw lines to match each word with its meaning in the text.

gliding	commotion
pauses	zooming
kerfuffle	fearless
intrepid	withdraws
hurtling	hesitates
sanctuary	minuscule
tiny	refuge
retreats	sliding

/8

Score: _____   **Time taken:** _____   **Target met?** _____

English Rapid Tests 4

Section 2 Test 5

Grammar and punctuation

Target time: 10 minutes

1. Write the correct auxiliary verb on the line to complete each sentence.

    Example: Marcia _was_ arguing with her sister throughout the film.

    a) Maddie _____ worked at the same school for 10 years.

    b) There _____ be a beautiful sunset this evening.

    c) We _____ still reading, even though it is bedtime.

    d) Fionne's legs _____ shaking with fear.

    e) I most certainly _____ not like mustard!

    f) Are you sure you _____ saved up enough money to pay for this?

    /6

2. Write out each sentence on the line, inserting dashes or commas to separate the extra information (parenthesis) from the rest of the sentence.

    Example: Surinder's mother who was a firefighter was at work.
    Surinder's mother, who was a firefighter, was at work.

    a) The cake which was very sticky tasted delicious.
    _____

    b) Lila's brother who goes to university will be home for the summer.
    _____

    c) The theme park which had more than 30 rides was an exciting day out.
    _____

    d) She put all her PE kit trainers, T-shirt and shorts into her bag.
    _____

    /4

Grammar and punctuation

Section **2** Test **5**
continued

3. Write out each phrase on the line, using an apostrophe to show possession.

Example: the kindness of the woman   the woman's kindness

a) the plane belonging to the girl   _____

b) the buzzing of the bees   _____

c) the happiness of the children   _____

d) the hat belonging to Carlos   _____

/4

4. Write the correct possessive pronoun on the line to complete each sentence.

Example: That bag belongs to you. It is yours.

a) Those cakes belong to James. They are _____.

b) That trophy belongs to Sarah. It is _____.

c) This coat belongs to me. It is _____.

d) That house is where we live. It is _____.

/4

5. Add a prefix to the words in bold below so that the sentence makes sense. Choose from the following prefixes: **auto–**, **re–**, **super–** and **inter–**. Write the prefix on the line. You may use each one only once.

Example: Mia had to _re_ **fresh** her computer screen.

a) Anna felt _____ **juvenated** after her day of rest.

b) "It's my turn to talk," _____ **jected** the speaker.

c) Many famous people write _____ **biographies**.

d) He needed _____ **human** strength to lift the heavy cabinet.

/4

| Score: | Time taken: | Target met? |

English Rapid Tests 4

25

Section 2 Test 6

Spelling and vocabulary

Target time: 10 minutes

1. Underline the word in each set of brackets that is a synonym of the word in bold.

   Example: fast   (slow   <u>quick</u>   feet)

   a) **desire**   (hate   crave   cult)

   b) **feign**   (collapse   ill   pretend)

   c) **flamboyant**   (floating   flammable   ostentatious)

   d) **submissive**   (passive   strong   dismissive)

   e) **arson**   (acrid   rob   torching)

   f) **miscellaneous**   (anonymous   various   many)

   /6

2. One word in each set does not go with the others. Underline this odd word out.

   Example: night   evening   dusk   <u>day</u>

   a) bracelet   gem   necklace   ring

   b) carnival   fair   swings   fête

   c) equilateral   quadrilateral   scalene   isosceles

   d) hen   kiwi   flamingo   platypus

   /4

3. Write out each abbreviation below in full on the line.

   Example: Dr   _Doctor_

   a) d.o.b.   _____

   b) dept.   _____

   c) e.g.   _____

   d) Oct.   _____

   /4

Spelling and vocabulary

Section **2** Test **6**
continued

4. One word from the first set of brackets goes together with one word from the second set of brackets to make a new word. Underline the two words and write the new word on the line.

Example: (<u>in</u> out about)   (<u>to</u> game of)   <u>into</u>

a) (van truck car)   (dog pet driver)   _____

b) (post letter stamp) (age write old)   _____

c) (does did do)   (at or it)   _____

d) (coffee tea sugar)   (loop round ring)   _____

/4

5. Some of the following sentences contain a spelling error. If you spot an error, circle the letter above it and write the correct spelling on the line. If there is no error, write **no error** on the line.

a)
A	B	C	D	E
Doctors keep	information	regarding	their patients	confidentiel.

_____

b)
A	B	C	D	E
Leprechauns	are thought	to be	extremely	mischivous.

_____

c)
A	B	C	D	E
Was this	evening's	dinner	sufficiently	nourishing?

_____

d)
A	B	C	D	E
The	librarian	recomended	several	books.

_____

/4

Score: Time taken: Target met?

English Rapid Tests 4   27

Section 3 Test 1

Comprehension

Target time: 10 minutes

Read the text and answer the questions below.

Extract from **Five Children and It**, *by E. Nesbit*

The children stood round the hole in a ring, looking at the creature they had found. It was worth looking at. Its eyes were on long horns like a snail's eyes, and it could move them in and out like telescopes; it had ears like a bat's ears, and its tubby body was shaped like a spider's and covered with thick soft fur; its legs and arms were furry too, and it had hands and feet like a monkey's.

5 "What on earth is it?" Jane said. "Shall we take it home?"

The thing turned its long eyes to look at her, and said – "Does she always talk nonsense, or is it only the rubbish on her head that makes her silly?"

It looked scornfully at Jane's hat as it spoke.

"She doesn't mean to be silly," Anthea said gently; "we none of us do, whatever you may think! Don't be frightened; we
10 don't want to hurt you, you know."

"Hurt *me*!" it said. "*Me* frightened? Upon my word! Why, you talk as if I were nobody in particular." All its fur stood out like a cat's when it is going to fight.

"Well," said Anthea, still kindly, "perhaps if we knew who you are in particular we could think of something to say that wouldn't make you angry. Everything we've said so far seems to have done so. Who are you? And don't get angry!
15 Because really we don't know."

"You don't know?" it said. "Well, I knew the world had changed – but – well, really – do you mean to tell me seriously you don't know a Psammead when you see one?"

"A Sammyadd? That's Greek to me."

"So it is to everyone," said the creature sharply. "Well, in plain English, then, a *Sand-fairy*. Don't you know a Sand-fairy
20 when you see one?"

It looked so grieved and hurt that Jane hastened to say, "Of course I see you are, *now*. It's quite plain now one comes to look at you."

"You came to look at me, several sentences ago," it said crossly, beginning to curl up again in the sand.

"Oh – don't go away again! Do talk some more," Robert cried. "I didn't know you were a Sand-fairy, but I knew directly I
25 saw you that you were much the wonderfullest thing I'd ever seen."

The Sand-fairy seemed a shade less disagreeable after this.

Write **A**, **B**, **C** or **D** on the answer line.

1. Why was the creature 'worth looking at' (line 1)?
   A It was very small.
   B It looked unusual.
   C It was fierce.
   D It was from Greece.

   _____ /1

2. What did Jane have on her head?
   A a ribbon
   B some rubbish
   C a hat
   D nothing

   _____ /1

3. Which word is a synonym for 'scornfully'?
   A mindfully
   B disdainfully
   C scorching
   D painfully

   _____ /1

4. How did the creature react to Anthea telling it not to be frightened?
   A It was offended.
   B It was very grateful.
   C It was sad.
   D It was confused.

   _____ /1

Comprehension

Section 3 Test 1
continued

5. Write <u>two</u> words to describe how you think the children must have felt when they first saw the creature.

   _____ and _____   /2

6. a) What did the creature first tell the children it was?

   _____

   b) What was the English version of its name?

   _____   /2

7. Look at the lines 16–20. Why do you think the creature seemed surprised that the children did not know what it was?

   _____
   _____
   _____
   _____   /4

8. Write <u>two</u> words that you think best describe Anthea's personality.

   _____ and _____   /2

9. Do you think Jane recognised the creature to be a Sand-fairy once it had told them what it was? Explain your answer.

   _____
   _____
   _____
   _____   /4

10. Why did the Sand-fairy seem 'less disagreeable' after Robert had spoken?

    _____
    _____
    _____
    _____   /4

Score: _____   Time taken: _____   Target met? _____

English Rapid Tests 4

Section 3 Test 2

Grammar and punctuation

Target time: **10 minutes**

1. Each sentence below is missing <u>two</u> items of punctuation. Write out each sentence on the line, adding in the correct punctuation.

   Example: Its sunny outside   <u>It's sunny outside.</u>

   a) Remember your glasses! her mother shouted after her.
   _____

   b) she had chosen a title for her novel 'The True Story of Louisa'.
   _____

   c) "Whose pen is this?" asked Beth. It's Lauren's, replied Callum.
   _____

   d) "Dont let me forget," James said. "The appointments at 5.00 p.m. today."
   _____
   _____

   /4

2. The words in the sentences below have been jumbled up and an extra word has been added in that is not needed. Unjumble the sentence in your head so it makes sense and write the extra word on the line.

   Example: When start the we do?   <u>the</u>

   a) secondary to turbulent teach The transition school Molly was for. _____

   b) the took afternoon park They the to and played toddlers old all. _____

   c) "today impeccably you Will behave?" mother asked their garden. _____

   d) become ever to radio was Leela's a host ambition show. _____

   e) They went pub the nobody beef for to so lunch that had to wash up. _____

   f) my pizza chicken and vegetable favourite Mushrooms are toppings. _____

   /6

30   Schofield & Sims

Grammar and punctuation

Section **3** Test **2**
continued

3. Read the sentences below. Identify the word classes of the words in bold in each sentence and write them on the lines.

   Example: Maryam **often rode** her bicycle into town.   _adverb_   _verb_

   a) **Canberra** is **the** capital city of Australia.   _____ _____

   b) Caitlin and her family **always** go on **exotic** holidays.   _____ _____

   c) The ride was **simultaneously** terrifying and **exhilarating**.   _____ _____

   d) She was the most **talented** dancer **in** the show.   _____ _____

   /4

4. Underline the verb in each group of words.

   Example: terror <u>terrify</u> terrible

   a) strong   stronger   strengthen

   b) drama   dramatise   dramatic

   c) solidify   solid   solidity

   d) activity   activate   active

   /4

5. Insert brackets into each sentence so that the sentence makes sense.

   Example: Aby **(**the girl I sit next to in class**)** lent me a pencil.

   a) Ravi asked Mrs Grant his next-door neighbour if she would sponsor him.

   b) Archie's cats Jessie and Alf are very friendly.

   c) My cousin who is two years older than me is coming to stay next week.

   d) Mason's mum who tends to worry a lot told him not to be late home.

   /4

   Score: ☐   Time taken: ☐   Target met? ☐

English Rapid Tests 4

Section 3 Test 3

Spelling and vocabulary

Target time: 10 minutes

1. Find one word that can be added before or after all four words below to make four new words. Write each new word on the line.

   a) force _____

   b) wood _____

   c) top _____

   d) home _____

   /4

2. Two of the words in each set do not go with the other three. Underline these <u>two</u> words.

   Example: dark <u>bright</u> gloomy <u>light</u> dusky

   a) tiger penguin bear zebra ostrich

   b) January October June March July

   c) lilac sapphire cobalt maroon azure

   d) sow mare doe boar ram

   /4

3. Add a prefix to the beginning of each word to change it into its antonym (opposite). Write the new word on the line.

   Example: ___hook ⟶ <u>unhook</u>

   a) ___characteristic ⟶ _____

   b) ___convenient ⟶ _____

   c) ___rational ⟶ _____

   d) ___typical ⟶ _____

   /4

Spelling and vocabulary

Section 3 Test 3
continued

4. Some of the following sentences contain a spelling error. If you spot an error, circle the letter above it and write the correct spelling on the line. If there is no error, write **no error** on the line.

a)
A	B	C	D	E
The puppy	was inevitably	getting up	to her usual	mischeif!

_____

b)
A	B	C	D	E
I had lots	of foreine	currency	left over from	holiday.

_____

c)
A	B	C	D	E
Did you	remember	to ask for	a receipt	for the petrol?

_____

d)
A	B	C	D	E
I felt	incredibly	releaved to	have survived	the accident.

_____

/4

5. Draw lines to match each word with its definition.

punctual   keeping someone or something within limits

idle   having a sweet or pleasant smell

confine   a difficult or painful experience

famine   happening or doing something at the appointed time

fragrant   a severe shortage of food

ordeal   avoiding work

/6

Score: ____ Time taken: ____ Target met? ____

Section 3 Test 4

Comprehension

Target time: 10 minutes

Read the text and answer the questions below.

From a Railway Carriage, by Robert Louis Stevenson

Faster than fairies, faster than witches,
Bridges and houses, hedges and ditches;
And charging along like troops in a battle,
All through the meadows the horses and cattle:
5 All of the sights of the hill and the plain
Fly as thick as driving rain;
And ever again, in the wink of an eye,
Painted stations whistle by.

Here is a child who clambers and scrambles,
10 All by himself and gathering brambles;
Here is a tramp who stands and gazes;
And here is the green for stringing the daisies!
Here is a cart run away in the road
Lumping along with man and load;
15 And here is a mill, and there is a river:
Each a glimpse and gone for ever!

Write **A**, **B**, **C** or **D** on the answer line.

1. What does this poem describe?
   A the advantages of travelling by train
   B sights that can be seen on a train journey
   C different types of transport
   D the dangers of rail travel

   _____ /1

2. Which two types of animal does the poet see from the train?
   A dogs and cats
   B mice and rabbits
   C horses and cows
   D pigs and sheep

   _____ /1

3. In line 10, what is the child doing?
   A picking blackberries
   B playing with a friend
   C waving at the train
   D riding in a cart

   _____ /1

4. Which word is a synonym for 'gazes'?
   A eats
   B stares
   C frowns
   D shouts

   _____ /1

34

Schofield & Sims

Comprehension

Section 3 Test 4 continued

5. Explain the meaning of line 12: 'And here is the green for stringing the daisies!'.

_____

_____ /2

6. What are the last two things that the poet sees from the railway carriage?

_____ and _____ /2

7. How does the rhythm of the poem add to the reader's experience?

_____

_____ /2

8. Read the last line of the poem. Explain in your own words what this means.

_____

_____ /2

9. Reread verse 1. Find two similes and write them on the lines.

_____

_____ /4

10. In the following passage, the words in bold have some missing letters. Fill in the letters of these incomplete words so that the passage makes sense.

A train is **a) t___ ___ ___cally** made up of an engine (also called a locomotive) to which **b) carr___ ___ ___es** or trucks are attached. The first steam locomotive was built in the United Kingdom in 1801 by Richard Trevithick, an English **c) en___ ___ ___eer** born in Cornwall. The first train tracks were made of wood, but metal was soon used instead since engines were so heavy.

Although trains were initially used to pull cargo, they were soon adapted to **d) tra___ ___ ___ort** people. Modern-day trains are usually powered by **e) elect___ ___ ___ity** or diesel. Trains are built to suit their **f) envi___ ___ ___ments** (for example, trains that cross mountains are constructed differently to those that travel on flat ground). /6

Score: _____   Time taken: _____   Target met? _____

English Rapid Tests 4

35

Section 3 Test 5

Grammar and punctuation

Target time: 10 minutes

1. In each sentence below, there are <u>two</u> punctuation errors. Underline the errors and then write the correctly punctuated sentence on the line.

   Example: The children all <u>=</u> six of them had <u>=</u> vanished!
   <u>The children – all six of them – had vanished!</u>

   a) She could only Play at, weekends.

   _____

   b) There were, sheep goats pigs and, dogs on the farm.

   _____

   c) Sadiq enquired. "Would you like some cake!"

   _____

   d) Her shopping list read tomatoes: red, onions and cheese.

   _____

   e) My friend Annie whom (I have known since) birth is coming to stay.

   _____

   f) The car engine revved loudly she pulled, out of the Space, and they were off!

   _____

   _____

   /6

2. Decide which of the words in bold completes the sentence using Standard English. Underline the word.

   Example: Zane did **good** / <u>**well**</u> in his maths test.

   a) She **done** / **did** all her homework carefully.

   b) You **were** / **was** top of the class!

   c) Hand me **them** / **those** keys.

   d) Aisha always eats **healthily** / **healthy**.

   /4

36   Schofield & Sims

Grammar and punctuation

Section 3 Test 5 continued

3. Turn each verb into a noun or adjective by removing or changing the suffix. Write the new word and its word class on the lines. There may be more than one possible answer.

   Example: terrify ⟶ terror   abstract noun

   a) simplify ⟶ _____ _____

   b) sympathise ⟶ _____ _____

   c) beautify ⟶ _____ _____

   d) shorten ⟶ _____ _____

   /4

4. The words in the following sentences have been jumbled up and an extra word has been added in that is not needed. Unjumble the sentence in your head so it makes sense and write the extra word on the line.

   Example: When start the we do?   the

   a) freezing The goggles didn't we was for long so pool swim. _____

   b) Grace field shouted, "Wait me for!" as they through ran the tree. _____

   c) moving Is further it Earth that the is Sun true from science the? _____

   d) flavour My favourite chocolate cream melt of chip ice is. _____

   /4

5. Add a prefix to the beginning of each word to change its meaning. Write the new word on the line. There may be more than one possible answer.

   Example: ___ behave ⟶ misbehave

   a) ___ turn ⟶ _____

   b) ___ count ⟶ _____

   c) ___ lead ⟶ _____

   d) ___ body ⟶ _____

   /4

   Score: ____   Time taken: ____   Target met? ____

English Rapid Tests 4

Section 3 Test 6

Spelling and vocabulary

Target time: 10 minutes

1. Underline the two words (one in each set of brackets) that are synonyms.

    Example: (<u>chilly</u> breeze windy)   (frosty hot <u>cold</u>)

    a) (idea inconceivable belief)   (overthink irreconcilable unthinkable)

    b) (ale wellness ailment)   (illness wounded skilful)

    c) (laser surgeon incision)   (graze incite cut)

    d) (rank jeopardise caress)   (harm endanger animalistic)

    /4

2. Decide which of the homophones in bold is the correct word for each sentence. Underline the word.

    Example: They saw a **heard / <u>herd</u>** of cows in the field.

    a) The boat was completely **stationery / stationary**.

    b) The author of Charlie's favourite book was his **idle / idol**.

    c) A perfect cup of tea has to be well **brewed / brood**.

    d) Sasha received lots of **complements / compliments** about her dress.

    /4

3. Underline the two words (one in each set of brackets) that are antonyms (opposites).

    Example: (chilly <u>hot</u> frosty)   (windy icy <u>cold</u>)

    a) (upbeat enthusiasm boredom)   (indifference essence grand)

    b) (promise truthful accept)   (intermittent vow dishonest)

    c) (colleague evil foe)   (nemesis friend spouse)

    d) (agree law obey)   (abstain serve defy)

    /4

38

Schofield & Sims

Spelling and vocabulary

Section **3** Test **6**
continued

4. Write out the words in each row on the line so that they are in alphabetical order.

   Example: ring ran run ruin race   race ran ring ruin run

   a) laugh life lose laughter loose

   _____

   b) train terrify trailer transistor terrible

   _____

   c) unusual unexpected until unto under

   _____

   d) zealot zeal zebra zealous zero

   _____

/4

5. Finish the incomplete words in each sentence by writing the missing letters in the gaps.

   Example: They went to a **res** _t_ _a_ _u_ **rant** to celebrate Michael's birthday.

   a) The **e** ___ ___ ___**tor** divides the Earth into the Northern and Southern Hemispheres.

   b) My father left a note for me on the table, but his writing was almost **illeg** ___ ___ ___**e**.

   c) Tara's brother went for a job **inter** ___ ___ ___**w** today.

   d) My mother works for an **interna** ___ ___ ___**nal** airline.

   e) Ivy's shoes were so tight, they almost cut off the **c** ___ ___ ___**ulation** to her toes.

   f) When they were playing in the garden yesterday afternoon, Louis and Joshua found an enormous **c** ___ ___ ___**ipede** under a rock.

/6

Score: Time taken: Target met?

English Rapid Tests 4   39

Progress chart

Write the score (out of 22) for each test in the box provided on the right of the graph.
Then colour in the row next to the box to represent this score.

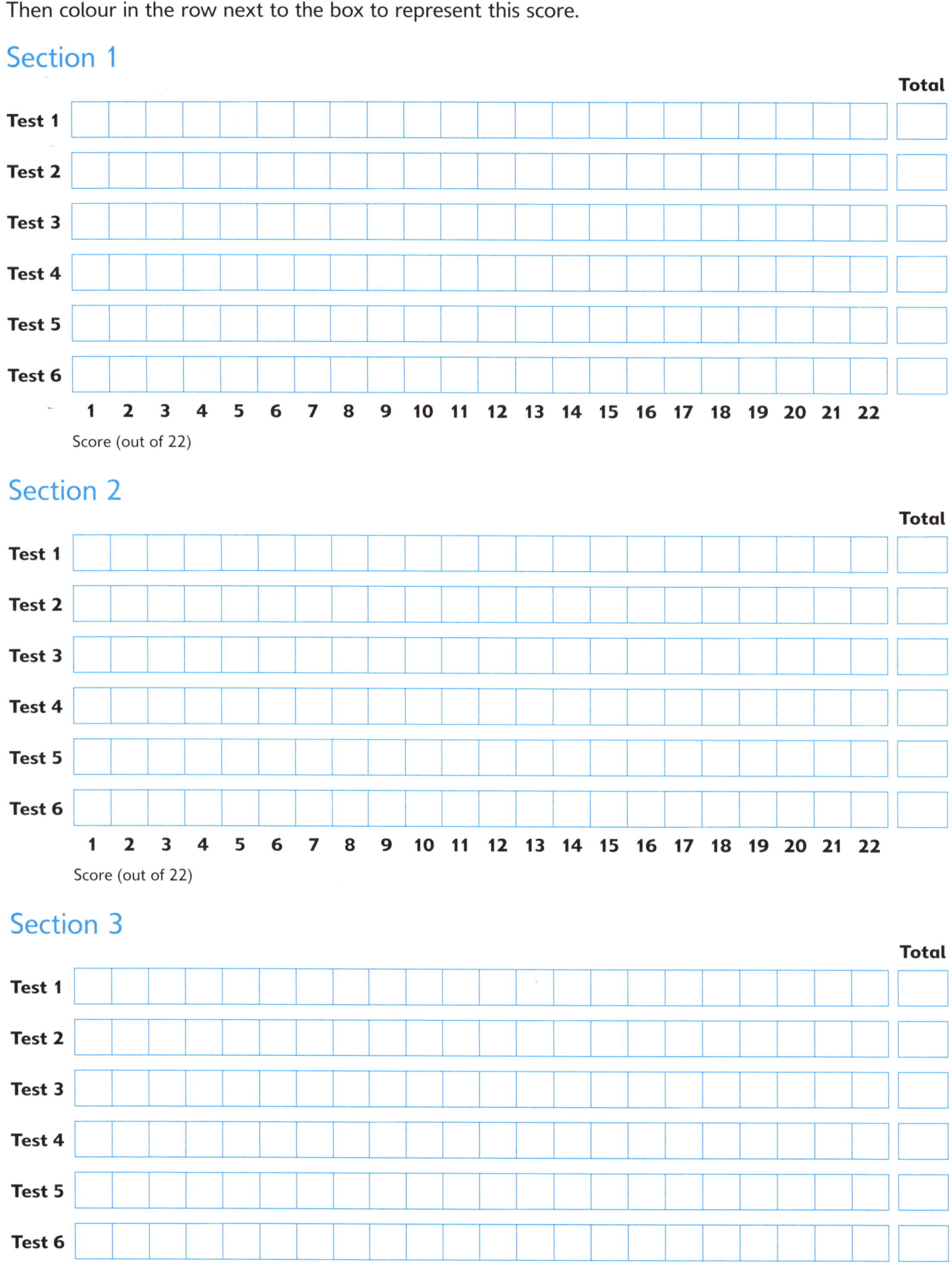

Section 1

| | | | | | | | | | | | | | | | | | | | | | | | Total |

Test 1
Test 2
Test 3
Test 4
Test 5
Test 6

1 2 3 4 5 6 7 8 9 10 11 12 13 14 15 16 17 18 19 20 21 22
Score (out of 22)

Section 2

Total

Test 1
Test 2
Test 3
Test 4
Test 5
Test 6

1 2 3 4 5 6 7 8 9 10 11 12 13 14 15 16 17 18 19 20 21 22
Score (out of 22)

Section 3

Total

Test 1
Test 2
Test 3
Test 4
Test 5
Test 6

1 2 3 4 5 6 7 8 9 10 11 12 13 14 15 16 17 18 19 20 21 22
Score (out of 22)